What Is an Amphibian?

by Lola M. Schaefer

red-spotted newt

Consulting Editor: Gail Saunders-Smith, Ph.D.

Consultant: Dwight Lawson, Ph.D.
General Curator, Zoo Atlanta

Pebble Books

an imprint of Capstone Press
Mankato, Minnesota

Pebble Books are published by Capstone Press
151 Good Counsel Drive, P.O. Box 669, Mankato, Minnesota 56002
http://www.capstone-press.com

1 2 3 4 5 6 06 05 04 03 02 01

Library of Congress Cataloging-in-Publication Data
Schaefer, Lola M., 1950–
    What is an amphibian?/by Lola M. Schaefer.
    p. cm.—(The Animal Kingdom)
    Includes bibliographical references (p. 23) and index.
    ISBN 0-7368-0863-9
    1. Amphibians—Juvenile literature. [1. Amphibians.] I. Title. II. Series.
QL644.2 .S33   2001
597.8—dc21

00-009667

Summary: Simple text and photographs present amphibians and their
general characteristics.

Note to Parents and Teachers

The Animal Kingdom series supports national science standards
related to the diversity of living things. This book describes and
illustrates the characteristics of amphibians. The photographs
support early readers in understanding the text. The repetition of
words and phrases helps early readers learn new words. This book
also introduces early readers to subject-specific vocabulary words,
which are defined in the Words to Know section. Early readers may
need assistance to read some words and to use the Table of
Contents, Words to Know, Read More, Internet Sites, and
Index/Word List sections of the book.

Table of Contents

leopard frog

caecilian

Amphibians are part
of the animal kingdom.
Amphibians can live
on land or in water.

Amphibians are cold-blooded. Their body temperature is the same temperature as their surroundings.

American toad

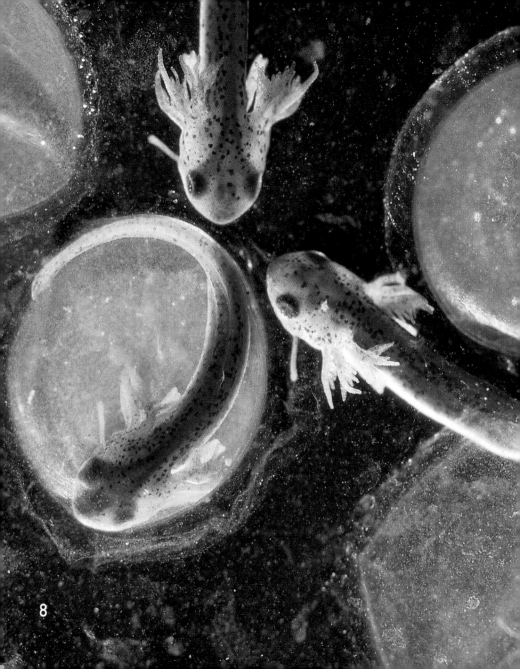

8

Most young amphibians hatch from eggs.

young salamanders

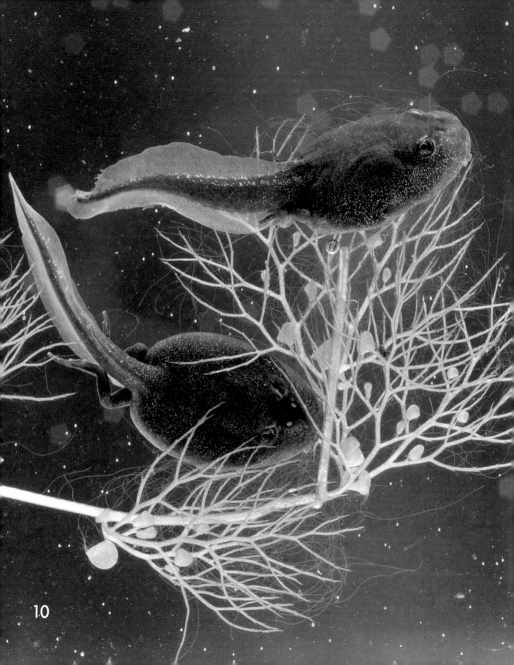

10

Most young amphibians change in size and shape to become adults.

American toad tadpoles

Young amphibians use gills to breathe underwater.

young spotted salamander

Most adult amphibians use lungs to breathe on land.

grey tree frog

Amphibians have mucus
on their skin.

fire salamander

Amphibians have
a skeleton.

small-mouthed salamander

Amphibians move in different ways. Some dig. Some crawl. Some slither. And some jump.

leopard frog

Words to Know

adult—an animal that is fully grown

animal kingdom—the group that includes all animals

breathe—to take oxygen into the body; oxygen is a gas found in air and water.

cold-blooded—having a body temperature that is the same as the temperature of the surroundings; fish, reptiles, and amphibians are cold-blooded animals.

gill—a body part used to take oxygen from water; tadpoles and young salamanders live underwater and use gills to breathe.

lung—a body part in the chest that animals use to breathe

mucus—sticky, wet liquid made by glands to protect parts of the body; amphibians use mucus to protect their skin and keep it moist.

skeleton—a framework of bones in a body

slither—to move by slipping and sliding

Read More

MacLeod, Beatrice. *Amphibians.* Wonderful World of Animals. Milwaukee: Gareth Stevens, 1997.

Savage, Stephen. *Amphibians.* What's The Difference? Austin, Texas: Raintree Steck-Vaughn, 2000.

Theodorou, Rod. *Amphibians.* Animal Babies. Des Plaines, Ill.: Heinemann Library, 2000.

Internet Sites

Amphibians
http://www.EnchantedLearning.com/coloring/amphibians.shtml

Amphibians on Critter Corner
http://www.dnr.state.wi.us/org/caer/ce/eek/nature/critteramph.htm

Animal Facts: Amphibians
http://www.fonz.org/animals/af-amphibians.htm

Classifying Critters
http://www.hhmi.org/coolscience/critters/critters.html

Index/Word List

adult, 11, 15
animal
  kingdom, 5
body, 7
breathe, 13, 15
change, 11
cold-blooded, 7
crawl, 21
different, 21
dig, 21
eggs, 9

gills, 13
hatch, 9
jump, 21
land, 5, 15
live, 5
lungs, 15
most, 9, 11, 15
move, 21
mucus, 17
shape, 11
size, 11

skeleton, 19
skin, 17
slither, 21
surroundings, 7
temperature, 7
underwater, 13
use, 13, 15
water, 5
ways, 21
young, 9, 11, 13

Word Count: 85
Early-Intervention Level: 11

Editorial Credits

Mari C. Schuh, editor; Kia Bielke, cover designer and illustrator; Marilyn Moseley LaMantia, illustrator (page 14); Kimberly Danger, photo researcher

Photo Credits

Dwight R. Kuhn, 1, 8, 12
Gary Meszaros/Bruce Coleman Inc., 6, 18
GeoIMAGERY/Frederic B. Siskind, 14
Hans Reinhard/Bruce Coleman Inc., cover (upper left)
Janis Burger/Bruce Coleman Inc., cover (lower right)
Joe McDonald/McDonald Wildlife Photography, 4 (bottom)
Kim Taylor/Bruce Coleman Inc., 10
Michael Fogden/Bruce Coleman Inc., cover (lower left), 16
M. P. L. Fogden/Bruce Coleman Inc., 4 (top)
Visuals Unlimited/G. and C. Merker, cover (upper right); Joe McDonald, 20